GIAN PAOLO BARBIERI

MADAGASCAR

THE HARVILL PRESS
LONDON

Conception and production
N P M PRODUCTION

Editorial Director
FABIO FASOLINI

Photographs
GIAN PAOLO BARBIERI
Assistants
ALAIN DITOMASO
MAURO MORI
FABIO RUSSO

Production & Co-ordination
CORRADO POZZOLI
Assistant
LUCIA NOGARA

Graphics
FELICE PERINI
Assistant
SUSAN OUBARI

Archival Research
LAURA VENTORUZZO
AURO VARANI

Anthropological Research
ROBERTO MATTEI

Annalisa Milella
Gian Franco Boveri, Honorary Consul of the Republic of Madagascar
Kodak Film
Studio Parolini Stampe Fotografiche
Madagascar Ministry of Culture
Police Department of Madagascar
Air Madagascar
Hotel Andilana Beach, Nosy-Be
Centre de Pêche Sportive de Madagascar, Nosy-Be
Sainte Marie Loisirs, Sainte Marie
Hotel Soanambo, Sainte Marie Island
Softline, Taomasina
Janette and Arman Rivert, Tuléar Hotel Plaza
Musée de l'Homme, Paris
Victoria and Albert Museum, London
Hirondelle Viaggi

From June to August 1994 I scoured Madagascar in all
directions, stopping on roads, in villages and markets in search
of subjects to photograph.

For almost every photograph I used a Linhof 4 x 5 on a tripod and
Polaroid 55 film which allows me instant control of the frames. For
pictures shot in Kodak 135 and 120 I used Rolliflex 6 x 6 and Canon.
I worked in every condition of light because the nature of the place and
the rhythms to which I worked gave me no chance to take my time.
I conceived the book in terms of that symbolic colour known as black. For
me black-and-white is an abstract term, all values are carried into it.
Through the life of Madagascar I tried to capture the decisive moment –
be it a moment of history or one of emotion and beauty. Occasionally
when I could no longer find the thing I had been on my way to
discovering, I would construct my picture and snap it the moment I had it
in the frame.

I tried to find my way into places I had chosen without any use of force.
I wanted to maintain the authenticity and spontaneity intact: respect for
the ambiance is the source out of which a style may develop. The choice
of lens was also determined by aesthetic considerations, which is why
I normally favoured the standard focus to achieve the greatest depth of
perspective; only occasionally did I resort to a telephoto lens for a portrait.

GIAN PAOLO BARBIERI

The grey matter of Madagascar; the photographs of Gian Paolo Barbieri

MICHEL TOURNIER

MADAGASCAR is sunflower seed, manioc, coffee. It is vanilla, redwood, a close relation of sandalwood, tree fern and orchids visited by huge butterflies. An amalgam of intense colours and powerful odours in a tropical climate with the seasons inverted in relation to our own (July in winter, January in summer) because here we are in the southern hemisphere.

A fine picture, and nothing of it survives in Gian Paolo Barbieri's photographs. No colours, no smells, no pungent flavours, no trace of the picturesque in these images, impressive though they are in their power and beauty. What is most striking is their perfection of form and their stern austerity. But in addition there is something else that arrests the attention. One word comes to mind, a ponderous, awkward term derived from Christian theology: consubstantiality. Indeed it is evident that these sands and these stretches of ground, the baobab woods, the chameleons' scales, the lacquered plumage of the ibis, the crododiles' claws, the smooth, muscular skin of the men, all these expressions of the reality of Madagascar clearly derive from the same substance. It is easy to see that the living spring is the same for frog, bird, and woman. All has been sculpted on the same day, formed out of the same matter, inspired with the same breath of life.

Black-and-white photography throws an admirable light on this consubstantiality of barks, skins, hides and scales. Let us pluck up the courage to propose this paradox: black-and-white photography comes

closer to reality than does the colour photograph because reality itself
is in black and white. The world around us is of itself colourless. It is
the painters that give it colour and if we believe we are seeing things in
colour it is only because we have spent too much time in art galleries and
picture exhibitions.

Besides, why keep harping on about black-and-white photography when it is
neither truly black nor white? Photography consists of a scale of greys, from
the lightest to the darkest, an ashen chiaroscuro to which we owe its depth
and subtlety. And that is not all . . . Goethe said that colours are the
sufferings endured by colourless light when it passes through turbid matter,
crystal, water or sky. So they manifest the loss of the primeval innocence of
light which, in "turbid matter", dissolves into the seven colours of the
rainbow corresponding to the seven deadly sins.

That is why this great island that Gian Paolo Barbieri offers us has such
a close resemblance to the Earthly Paradise of the Fall.

The grey substance of Madagascar is the original clay of Creation that
comes from the hand of God.

P.S. One of the most beautiful of these pictures shows us eight men
walking in the desert carrying a huge litter (reminiscent of a papal *sedia
gestatoria*), on which a woman of savage beauty sits clasping to herself two
small children. Confronted with this image many will be possessed by a
sense of *déjà vu.* That is certainly what happened to me . . . and I set off to

look. My search took me to the Musée d'Orsay, to the big painting of
"Cain" by Cormon, dated 1880 and inspired by Victor Hugo's poem
"*La Conscience*" in *La Légende des Siècles*. We recollect that Cormon was
one of the greatest and most meticulous representatives of the "Pompier"
school in the last century, whose masters were Horace Vernet, Neuville,
Luminais, Lecomte du Nouy, etc. This school cluttered the official
exhibitions with vast historical reconstructions, and the Impressionists had
to battle against them to achieve recognition; it has since fallen into a
largely unmerited disrepute. Perhaps the foregoing considerations may
shed a little light on the debate.

These "historical painters" undoubtedly possessed an astonishing
technique. They had frequented a school, and knew how to draw a horse,
a tree, a house and realise vast compositions that were at once dynamic
and well balanced. All this is fine and not to be underrated. Their weak
point was colour, and it was on this that the Impressionists defeated them.
They drew fantastically, then laboured to colour in what they had drawn.
The result was barely up to illustrating a school history textbook. To them
more than to anyone else the virtues of black and white should have been
preached, the subtleties of grey chiaroscuro, the firmness of a line.

Bibliography

ABINAL, R. P. , MALZAC, S. J.	*Dictionnaire Malgache-Français*, Tananarive 1899.
CALLET, R. P.	*Tantara ny Andriana eto Madagascar*, Tananarive 1908.
DAHL, O. Chr.	*Malgache et Maanjan*, Oslo 1951.
DEMPWOLF, O.	*Vergleichende Lautlehre des Austronesischen Wortschatzes, Dritter Band. Beihefte zur Zeitschrift für Eingeborenen Sprachen*, Berlin 1938.
FRAZER, J. G.	*The Golden Bough*, London 1911.
GENNEP, A. VAN	*Tabou et Totémisme à Madagascar*, Paris 1904.
LEHMANN, F. R.	*Die Polynesischen Tabusitten*, Leipzig 1930.
MALINOWSKI, B.	*Magic, Science and Religion*, Boston (Mass.) 1948.
MARETT, R. R.	*Tabu*, in *Encyclopædia of Religion and Ethics*, Edinburgh 1921.
ID.	*The Threshold of Religion*, London 1914.
MOLET, L.	*Le Bain Royal à Madagascar*, Tananarive 1956.
RICHARDSON, J.	*A new Malagasy-English Dictionary*, Antananarivo 1885.
RUSSILLON, H.	*Le Vintana ou sort*, in "Bulletin de l'Académie Malgache", Tananarive 1914.
RUUD, J.	*Guder og fedre*, Oslo 1947.
ID.	*Panthéon et religion chez les Tanala*, in "Bulletin de l'Académie Malgache", Tananarive 1954.
SÖDERBLOM, N.	*Gudstrons uppkomst*, Stockholm 1914 (German translation: Das Werden des Gottesglaubens, Leipzig 1916).
VIG, L.	*Skæbnelære og Dagvelgeri*, Aarhus 1905.

THE PHOTOGRAPHS

JUNE 1994. BAOBAB ON THE ROAD SOUTH
BETWEEN TULÉAR AND FORT DAUPHIN

2 SAINT AUGUSTIN. THE FISHERMEN CARRY THE FISH
ON TO THE BEACH FROM THE BOATS

NEAR THE TRAILS, IN THE MAHAFALY ZONE, THERE WERE
TOMBS PROTECTED BY THE ALOHALOS, WOODEN SCULPTURES
DISPLAYING THE LIVES OF THE DECEASED

NOON IN THE VILLAGE OF ANAKAO

MANDRARE. BEFORE MAN
THERE WAS FOREST THAT
WAS SACRIFICED TO
5   MAKE ROOM FOR
THESE ENDLESS ROWS
OF AGAVES

MORONDAVA. IN A PIROGUE
I FOUND THIS SAWFISH BEAK

10

MAJUNGA, AUGUST 1994.
THIS GATE IS OPENED EVERY SEVEN YEARS.
IT IS KNOWN AS THE GATE OF THE KING BECAUSE
WITHIN THE STOCKADE THERE IS A HUT WHICH KEEPS
THE GOLDEN URNS CONTAINING THE KINGS' ASHES

13 TAMPING DOWN THE RED-EARTH PATHS
AFTER THE GREAT RAINS

14 | TATTOOED FISHERMAN FROM RADAMA ISLAND

OVERLEAF
15 | EFOETSE. SALT LAGOON, FROM CORMON'S PAINTING
(PARIS, MUSÉE D'ORSAY);
RECONSTRUCTION OF MADAGASCAN LITTER

IN THE PARCHED SOUTH, ABSENCE OF SHADE IN
THE THORNY FOREST OF DIDIERAECEE

MAJUNGA SLAUGHTERHOUSE, AT DAWN

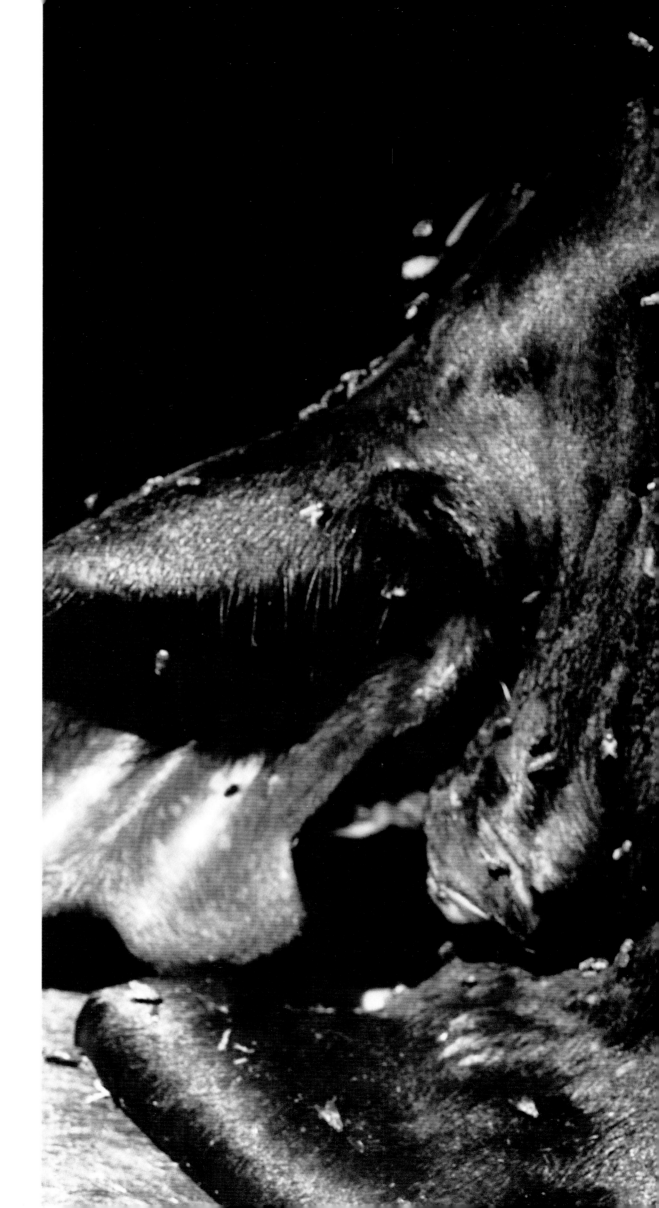

21   BANQUET FOR 'EYE-LICKER'
     FLIES AT THE BUTCHERS'

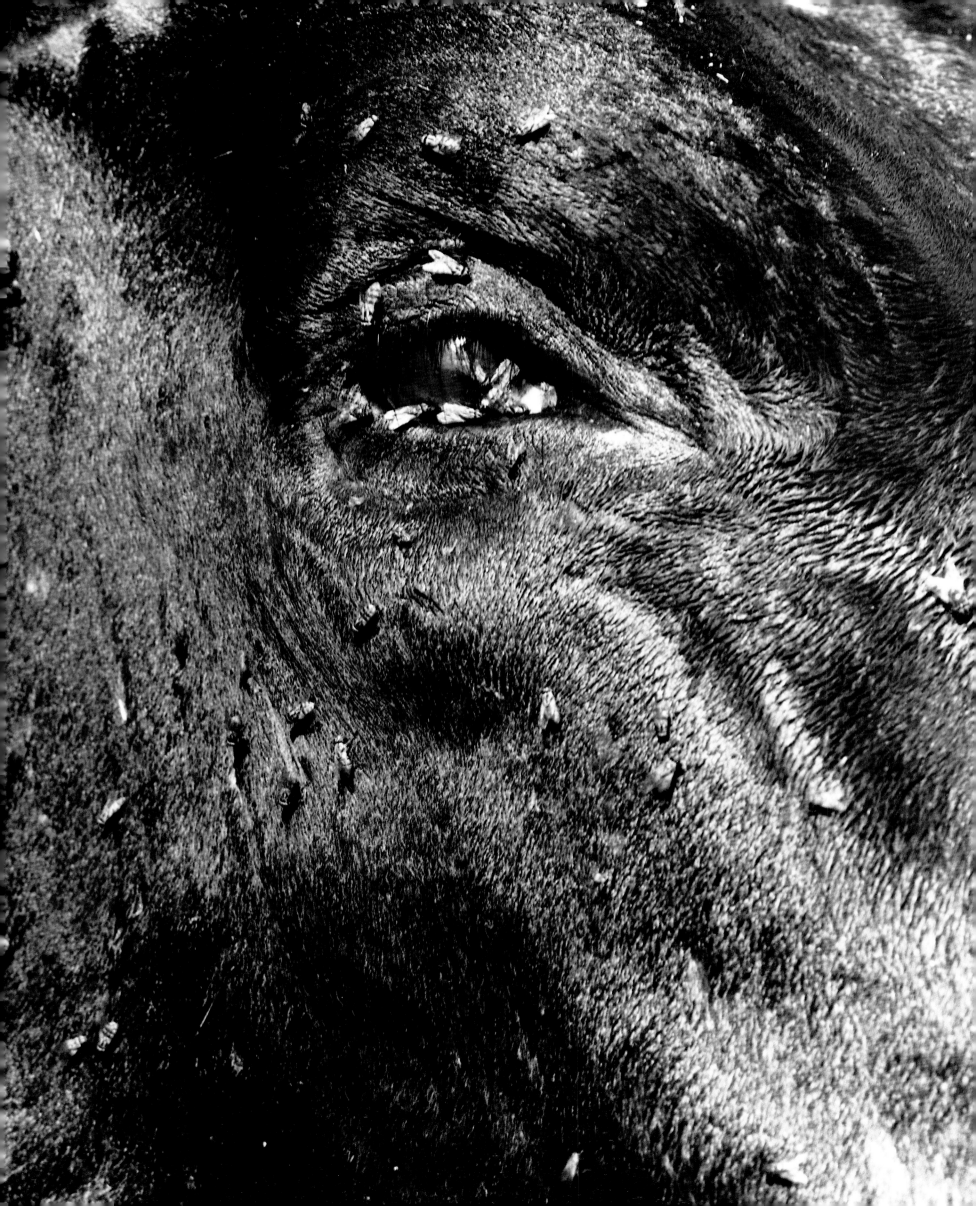

VEZO VILLAGE AT SUNDOWN. A FISHERMAN RESTING

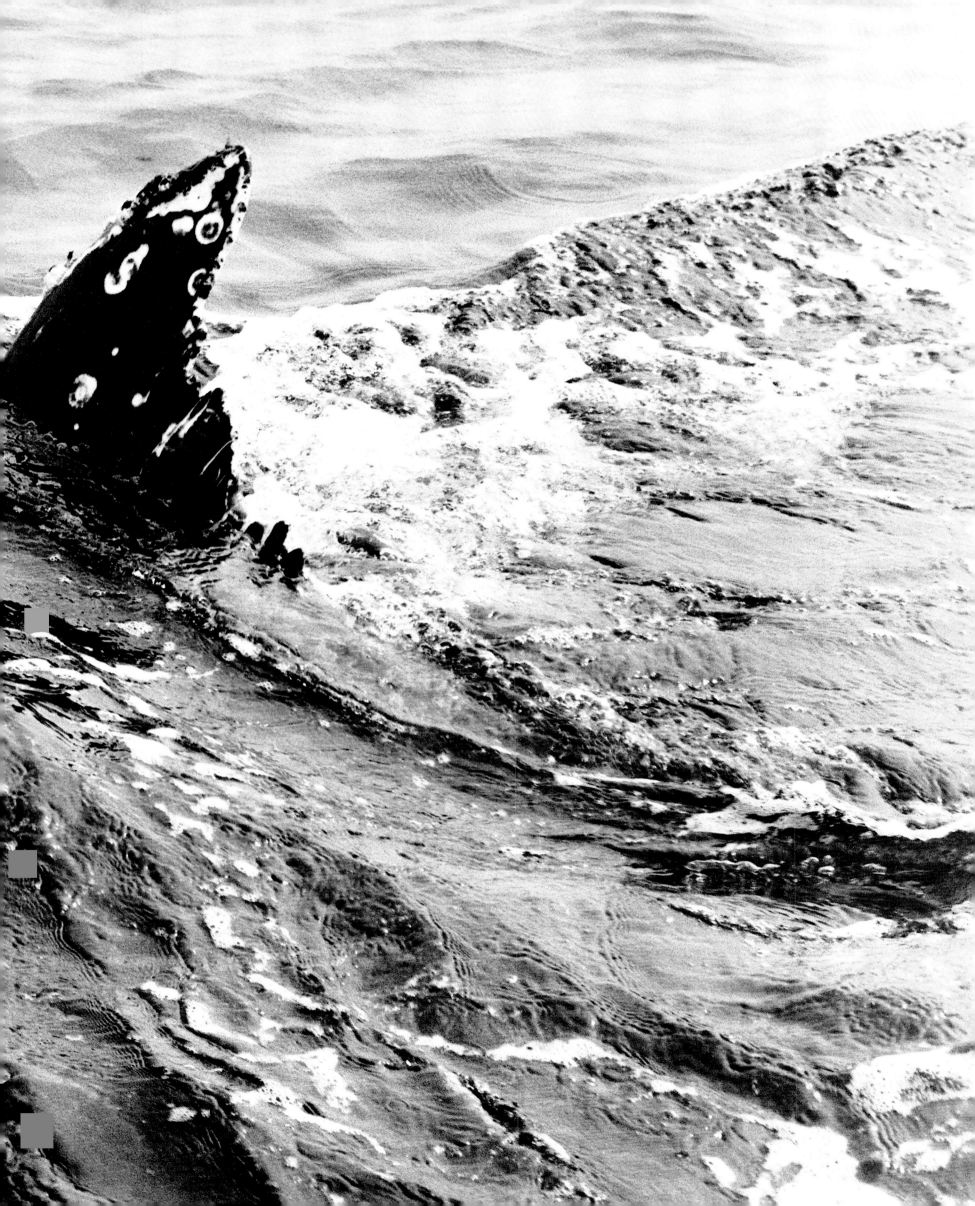

29 ANAKAO BEACH, VEZO VILLAGE.
A SHAMAN-FISHERMAN WITH YOUNG WIFE AND
WHALE'S VERTEBRA

PORT OF NOSY-BE. GIRL MET ON THE SHORE

ANTANKARANA. THE FEATURES OF THIS YOUNG MAN SUGGEST
WE ARE AT THE CROSSROADS OF ASIA, AFRICA AND ARABIA

SAINT AUGUSTIN. WHEN THE FISHING FLEET COMES IN
THE VEZOS SHARE OUT THE CATCH

LOKOBÉ. IN CERTAIN AREAS BOA CONSTRICTORS ARE OFTEN MET WITH; ALTHOUGH THEY ARE NON-POISONOUS, THEY ARE GREATLY FEARED BY THE MADAGASCANS

35   NOSY KOMBA. EACH FAMILY OWNS ITS FRACTION OF BEACH, WHERE IT
HAULS UP ITS PIROGUE AND DRIES ITS CATCH

40 | NOSY MANGABE. RAIN FOREST

OVERLEAF
41 | ANDASIBE, ON THE WAY TO TAMATAVA.
BENEATH A TROPICAL DOWNPOUR
THIS BOY IS CARRYING A HUGE TRAVELLERS' PALM FLOWER

NOSY MANGABE. THE MALE MACAO
LEMURS ARE COMPLETELY BLACK

AMBOASARI, WITCH DOCTOR ANTANDREY.
THEY ARE KNOWN AS MPISIKIDY AND THEY EFFECT CURES WITH SEEDS,
STONES AND HERBS KEPT IN A ZEBU'S HORN

AMBATOROA, TO THE NORTH OF SAINTE MARIE ISLAND

AMBATOROA. THE STATUES FACING SEAWARDS
REPRESENT THE EFFIGIES OF THE DEAD

TULÉAR. WORK ENDS AT THE SLAUGHTERHOUSE

47

BELO TSIRIBIHINA. RECONSTRUCTION
OF THE FUNERARY RITES PRACTISED
BY CERTAIN TRIBES.
THE KINSMEN WOULD FEAST
ON THE DECEASED PERSON'S FLESH
AND DRINK ITS LIQUIDS

BELO TSIRIBIHINA. THE BODY'S LIQUIDS ARE DRAINED OFF; THEY WILL
PURIFY THOSE WHO DRINK THEM AND TRANSMIT CERTAIN POWERS

49 AT PANGALANE. AS I WAITED FOR THE FERRY,
I SAW ON THE VERANDAH OF A HUT THIS MOTHER
WITH HER CHILD

MAJANGA. LOOKING OUT OF THE HOTEL WINDOW
I WAS STRUCK BY THIS PROCESSION OF POUS-POUS

SAINTE MARIE. AFTER THE FISHING I ASKED THIS YOUNG WOMAN TO POSE NUDE.
SHE AGREED READILY AND WITH A SMILE

DZAMANDAZAR. CRANES SHIFT MOUNTAINS
OF SUGAR-CANE TOWARDS THE DISTILLERY

54 TSIOMBE. ONE OF MADAGASCAR'S SEVEN SPECIES OF BAOBAB.
LEGEND HAS IT THAT ITS BEAUTY WAS AN AFFRONT TO THE GODS,
SO IT WAS PUNISHED BY CONCEALING ITS LUXURIANT LOCKS
UNDERGROUND AND SHOWING ITS BLACK ROOTS TO THE SKY

First published in 1994 by
Umberto Allemandi & C. SRL., Torino

First published in Great Britain in 1995 by
The Harvill Press
84 Thornhill Road
London N1 1RD

A CIP catalogue record for this book is
available from the British Library

ISBN 1 86046 085 2

Printed and bound in Italy by
Le Arti Grafiche Giacone, Torino